MOVING ON

First published in 1999 by
Marino Books
an imprint of Mercier Press
16 Hume Street Dublin 2
Tel: (01) 6615299; Fax: (01) 6618583
E.mail: books@marino.ie

© Rita Lawlor 1999

ISBN 1 86023 104 7

10 9 8 7 6 5 4 3 2 1

A CIP record for this title is available
from the British Library

Cover design by Penhouse Design
Printed in Ireland by ColourBooks,
Baldoyle Industrial Estate, Dublin 13

MOVING ON

RITA LAWLOR

to my family and friends

ACKNOWLEDGEMENTS

I'd like to thank all the people who helped with this book: Stephen Hennessy, who helped get information together; Yvonne Stewart, who helped with editing, research and typing; Rita Kwiotek, who helped to meet people about the book; Pádraig Ó Móráin from the *Irish Times*, who helped with advice; Máiríde Woods, who helped with my writing and made corrections; Philip Keogh, who helped me find someone to do the typing; Peter Knowles, a disabled person who helped me with the typing; Audrey Whelan, who helped me finish the typing; Mary McEvoy, who helped me write a letter to Marino Books; Mary Duffy, who helped get some of my story typed up for the 'Life' competition on Gay Byrne's radio show; and Rehab in Sandymount. I would also like to thank the people who gave their time to look at my work and all the other people, too many to name, who helped me.

PREFACE

This is how the book first started.

In 1994, when I was in the Dublin Self-Advocacy Group, we were sent a letter from the Louise Bashford Award about making a video. I really wanted to make a video, so I sent them my ideas. They liked my ideas but I hadn't been able to say how much it would cost to film them, so I didn't win. But I thought I'd go ahead anyway and write my story.

CONTENTS

Part III

Appendices

PART I

1

THE BEGINNING OF MY STORY

My name is Rita Lawlor. I was in the Dublin Self-Advocacy Group. I have a learning difficulty. Otherwise I am an able person and can speak up for myself. I work in the Gresham Hotel. I have been on television programmes like *Teletalk, Checkup,* and *Get a Life* and radio shows like *The Pat Kenny Show* and have been written about in the newspapers. People with disabilities are not children. We are adults who can express ourselves. I was born in 1957 in Newbridge Road in Naas, County Kildare, in a house across the road from where our family doctor lived. Mammy lived her whole life in that house. My five brothers and three sisters were there twenty years. I had a problem: I did not walk until I was about four years of age. I was brought down to the playpen in the yard, where Mrs Butler and Mrs Plant, who lived on either side of our house, and my grandaddy came to see me.

Mammy worked in Lawlors Hotel in Naas. She washed up in the kitchen and cleaned. Mammy once put me on the bed when the fire was lighting. I pulled feathers out of the mattress and put them into the fire and nearly set the house alight. In fact, I think the house did catch fire and my daddy saved me from it. Daddy, who was from Kerry, was a sergeant in the army in the Curragh in County Kildare. He was a driver and a driving instructor in the army and served in Ireland, the Congo and Cyprus. a good few years. He retired after twenty-one years in the army and now does things around the house like cooking the dinner and watching a lot of TV.

I used to kick people when I was walking down the road. When I was brought down the town in Naas I used to kick people going to Mass. Once I went down the town on my own, and my family went looking for me. My mother told me she brought me to Father Moore's Well when I could not walk and I was cured there.

I broke my cot as well. I was playing washing the clothes. My mother left me playing with the washing board. One night I was in bed and saw a big black spider on the windowsill. I screamed my head off. My mammy came in to me in the bedroom. I said, 'There's a big spider.' She took it up in a cloth. It was running around on the cloth and I was still screaming, looking at it on the cloth. So my mother let me go in with my brothers and sisters in the other bedroom. We all had great fun playing on the bed, lifting up the mattress and playing hide-and-go-seek and jumping on the bed.

When I was around five I was in ordinary school, the Sisters of Mercy primary school, in the convent near the church in Naas. I do not remember what I did in school because I was so young. I came home after school – it was a day school. The teacher in the school must have said to my mother that I was too slow to keep up with the others in class: she must have talked to the family doctor and my mother. So I was sent away by the doctor to a boarding school, St Theresa's in Blackrock, Dublin.

2
—

SCHOOL DAYS

I was six when I went to boarding school. I was crying for two weeks because I was so sad. I got on grand with the girls, except for the odd row.

The school was an all-girls place. I slept in a big dormitory with about forty other girls. The boarding school was divided into three groups. The groups were called Holy Angels, Juniors and Seniors. There were about forty children in each group. I was in the Holy Angels for a while, then I was put into the Juniors. All the groups had dormitories, dining rooms for eating and a day room for watching television and the other things people would do. In the dining room there were big, rectangular tables. The food was nice. Most days we had a different menu for dinner: stew, potatoes, vegetables, fish or meat and different desserts – rice, semolina and sago. Tea was eggs with bread or toast, beans and a fry. Breakfast was porridge or cornflakes.

The Daughters of Charity ran the school. Some staff slept in their own place in the school and some went home after work. One day one of the staff went to dry my hair with the hair dryer. I would not let her: I was terrified of it.

I was out of school for weeks because I fractured my shoulder when I was playing football in the school field. Sometimes the boys came in, and the nuns let them play football with us. The boys were nice; if they hadn't been, the nuns probably wouldn't have let them come up. The nun who had brought me to the hospital said 'I hope you are right about your shoulder'; I had had it X-rayed and my shoulder was bandaged up. I had to stay in bed all the time until I was better. When I asked the nun if I could have my dinner with the other girls in the dining room, she said, 'Yes, some day.' One of the girls used to tease me when I was in bed. I got up very slowly and pulled her dressing gown and ripped all the buttons off it. I got into trouble for that. As punishment, the nun would not let me have dinner with the other girls in the dining room. I made my Holy Communion and my Confirmation in the church in Blackrock village. I had a good day. My mother came up to bring me out for those two days.

I made my Holy Communion when I was eight and my Confirmation when I was around nine or ten. I think my mother brought me either home or into town. I had a good time. We had outings like going to the circus once a year. My parents came up to see me sometimes at weekends and sometimes my mother brought me home when she was not busy. By the time I was fourteen I used to do my washing in a small laundrette in the school. There was a staff member there who looked after the place and helped us with the washing machine and the clothes dryer if we needed it. Her name was Mrs Early; she was nice. Another girl, Liz, would get sweets when she came in from Mrs Early, and the girl used to give me a sweet. The staff in the laundrette were looking after the clothes of people from the chapel and other places.

One time I was waiting on the ambulance minibus to bring me home for Christmas. All the girls down my side of the dormitory were gone home except for me and another girl, so that night I went down to the other part of the dormitory and slept with another girl in her bed. All her part of the dormitory was full at the time. Then the next day I got smacked on my bum in the dining room at breakfast time for leaving my own bed. Another night I was talking to one of the girls in her bed when I thought of putting a pillow down my bed so that night the night nurse would think I was in bed.

There was a farm in the school. It was not too far from the prefab, where the TV room was. It was a small farm with big hens and chickens.

We used to have to get ready in the dormitory to go to church. When we were all ready, with our brightly coloured hats on, we had to wait for a while before the bell rang. We used to play with our hats, throwing them at each other. We went to Benediction and the Rosary most nights. We had to go to bed around nine o'clock every night. Some days after school we went to the TV room or played with the chestnut tree down the end of the tarmacadam not far from the playroom. We used to throw stones up at the tree to get the chestnuts down from it. Sometimes we went for a walk around the grounds in the school with the staff. When the weather was fine we went to the school field. In the field there were swings, a merry-go-round, bars and a glasshouse for tomatoes. We used to take a few tomatoes from the glasshouse and eat them. Sometimes we had homework from school to do, like spellings.

In school my uncle Con came up to see me once a week. He brought me up a lot a cakes. He was living in Dublin at the time, working in a bakery. Except for the times when he brought me out around Dublin, I was in the boarding school all the time. Now my uncle Con lives in Naas. I went out when the staff in the school brought us out. I went out some Sundays after dinner with the staff. The staff brought us to the sweet shop. I bought some sweets for my treat, like crisps and toffees. Some Sundays I watched TV after dinner. Sometimes we went to the park; I went on the swings.

I went swimming if the weather was good and the staff would bring us to the beach. The beach was only about ten minutes away. One day I had a choice of either doing Irish dancing or going swimming. I picked swimming. We were brought to the beach, the ones that wanted to come. When I went into the water I could not swim. Some of the girls were not pleased that I did not go to the Irish dancing. There was one night that one of the girls asked me to get her a drink of water. I went and got it. On my way back to the dormitory I saw the night nurse. I ran down under the bed but she caught me and I got into trouble. Another day one of the girls, Margaret, was having a party in bed and I joined her and we ate crisps and ice cream. I heard someone coming and, in a panic, I said to Margaret, 'What will I do?' I could do nothing, and the nun found me eating with the girl. I got smacked on the bum. A nun would slap our hands if we did anything wrong. That was not right.

One day in school I wanted to go to the toilet. I saw the principal nun, Sister Louise, who asked me where I was going. I said, 'I am going to the toilet.' I said I had told my teacher that I was going to the toilet, but by the time I was finished talking to the principal I went to the toilet in front of her. I do not remember what happened then. Perhaps that is just as well.

We had a Lions Club in the school. I remember getting wool they sent in for the girls. We did basketball at school with a basketball teacher. We also had a school sports day, where we did egg-and-spoon racing, sack racing and running all out in the field.

I did not like reading and spelling at school. One day in the classroom we were asked to spell 'grass'. I could not spell it and the teacher brought me into another classroom and said to the whole class, 'Rita cannot spell grass.' I felt sad.

During the break I used to play running with some of the girls. I enjoyed playing with them. One day at break time I was rolling around the bars in the playground and I fell off. I was a while on the ground and then I got up. Then there was another day I was rolling around on the bar and talking with a few girls. The nun thought I was saying something cheeky to her so she punished me by making me stand in the classroom with my face against the wall.

I used to go on my holidays to Newbridge Road. Vera, my auntie, lived at home in Naas. When she brought me out around Dublin my pants used to keep falling down. I had to keep pulling them up. I pulled them up on the street in front of people. My auntie Vera brought me to Dublin on the country bus when I was at home on holidays. She used to have parties at home. We had ice cream, sweets, crisps and tea. She was very good to us. My sister Mary, my friends and I used to play with the spinning top. Mary used to do crochet with her friend. I used to look at them all the time doing it. Then one day I tried it out. I kept trying all the time, making a square and a pouch. I used to put my money down my sock in my shoes. I used to get a good laugh about the money. My teeth used to fall out and my family would say, 'Put your tooth under your pillow' and I would get money. My auntie Vera used to say, 'Do a dance for the money', and I did. My auntie Vera lives in England now. My grandfather was good to me. When I went home for my holiday from school he gave me pocket money. My grandfather died in May 1976. My aunties, uncles and daddy gave me money and I used to put it down my sock.

When I went back to school after our holidays the nun would put our money away in the office to keep it safe. When we went out with the staff we would get our money from her.

When I was about ten I got my hair cut short. I used to put a rope on my head to make my hair long. Then my mother bought me a hair wig to make my hair seem long. Then my hair got long again, so I did not need the wig. I was still in school when my family moved to St Martin's Avenue in Naas. One time on my holidays, in the summer, when the weather was good, my sister Mary brought me and my two brothers to the lakes in Naas.

Some days when I was playing in the front garden a group of children would come to the gate of our house and tease me. I used to push them away. Each time I came home for my holidays from school I felt people were looking at me because I was travelling in a minibus. The children in the neighbourhood used to be looking at me getting into the minibus because it came from a special school.

Sometimes when I was at home on holidays mammy would bring me to raffles in Muley's pub in Naas. I was very lucky then: I used to win a lot – sometimes four or six times. I might win ham, drink, sweets or something like that. I would give them to mammy. I enjoyed the raffles: people in the pub would say to my mother that my hair was very long down my back and very nice. Now I do not like pubs, and I go to them very seldom when I come home. On the odd weekend mammy brought me home.

One day my sister Mary brought us to the lake in Naas and I floated in the water. Then I shouted, 'I can swim! I can swim!' Then I dived into the water and banged my knees off a rock and they bled. My sister Mary, our friends and I used to play catching bumble bees. We got them in a jar.

On Sundays we went to Mass in school after having breakfast: rashers, bread and tea. For dinner we had potatoes, meat, vegetables, and ice cream for dessert. After school we had cocoa. One day all the cups of cocoa were on the table and I was first down. I drank the whole lot – about thirty or forty cups – and got punished. They put me in the bathroom, where the staff were bathing somebody.

When I was in the classroom we had to wear gymslips.

Then after school we had to change out of our gymslips and get into our other clothes. We left our school books in the desks in the classroom; we had our own desks. We had PE in the assembly hall. I enjoyed the bars and going up the ropes.

We had plays for Christmas before our holidays. We had to practise for the plays. I was in the choir, where we sang hymns. Our parents usually came up to see us but there was one Christmas play which my mother did not come to. After the play was over I cried because my mammy was not there. Then one Christmas she came for the play and brought me home for the Christmas holidays.

It was good when Santa came to me on Christmas morning. I got my present. One Christmas I got a lovely big doll. I brought it to school and the nuns put it in the press for me to keep it safe. The doll had white long hair tied up in two ponytails with red ribbons, and she had blue eyes. The doll had a red-and-white-striped dress and white socks and black shoes.

Christmas is a time for peace and joy when Santa comes with presents for children, and it's nice when all the family gets together and sees each other to talk. It is the time the Lord was born. My family used to call me a glutton because I ate too much: it was a joke and we had laughs at it. I used to eat about five dinners or desserts.

One day my sister Mary brought us to the hay in the field and a dog was chasing me and I kept running around the pram and finally the dog got me and bit me. My sister Mary used to bring me and my brothers down to the wood around Cara Road. We swung on a big branch of a tree. We had great fun. I liked the craftwork, games, cookery and PE at school. When I was leaving school people were getting jobs and training to be in a flat by cooking potatoes, vegetables, meat and that kind of thing.

I left school at sixteen and went home to Naas for a while, where I used to play with the children. After dinner we played in the tarmacadam playground in St Martin's Avenue. We played games like running and chasing. We had great fun. Some nights I would watch TV – whatever my daddy had on. He would watch films; they were very good. When I was at home my daddy would have a lovely dinner for us. Most days we had different dinners: fish, fish fingers, potatoes, vegetables, meat, stew, steak-and-kidney pie, eggs and sometimes dessert, like rice, sago or custard. Then on Sundays at home we had potatoes, bacon and cabbage and sometimes custard or ice cream. For breakfast I would have cornflakes. For tea we had tea, beans and bread, fried white pudding, rashers and sausages. On Sunday morning Daddy did the fry. I was at home for a few months: I liked the food.

*

I bumped into Sister Louise around two years ago at a bus stop near where she lives. We were delighted to see each other again and I gave her a big hug. She brought me in for tea and cake in a restaurant, where she gave me her address and phone number. I wrote to her and sent her a Christmas card. She said we should meet again so I phoned her after Christmas and we made arrangements to meet in town. We went for tea and cake; then we were thinking what to do. So I asked her to come to my place and she did. She was pleased with it and said I had made the place lovely. Then that day we made arrangements to see each other again – when the weather was good I would come to St Vincent's on Navan Road.

At the end of April I rang her to ask her if I could come to St Vincent's. She said I could come and I got the bus up there. She met me and gave me tea and biscuits and we talked about old times at school. Then she showed me around the grounds. I saw the gardens, fields, swimming pool and bungalows, which are like small houses for people who cannot do things for themselves. It is a big place. Then we had a nice dinner: chicken, potatoes, cabbage and Mars ice cream. After dinner she showed me some photos of the school. We had a great day. When she was leaving me at the gate she was really funny.

We are children
with no voice
thise are childre playing games,

skipping

Thise is a
game 9 wate
a letter

going
up
tree.
for
the
rope
to get a down

3

THE LAUNDRY TIMES

After a few months it was arranged that I go to Sean McDermott Street Convent. It was run by the Daughters of Charity. I was a boarder there as well. I lived in the elderly women's section for about two years. I was in a big dormitory with my own cubicle. It was like a small bedroom with a curtain for a door. It was like an institution: we used to have to ring the bell to get in and out. Although it was a dangerous area, it was a good community.

I did not go out until Mary, one of the elderly women, started bringing me out. She showed me how to go out. She came with me and showed me around Dublin. She brought me out a lot and I got used to going out. Then I started going out on my own. Mary was a very nice person. I had fun with her. She is smaller than me and has blue eyes. I was grateful to her. She worked on the sewing machine in the office, mending clothes. I used to work in the laundry. The sheets would come off the presser and we would have to fold them. It was very warm there in the summer. It was all right, but I wouldn't like to work there all the time. We started work at nine o'clock and finished at about five. We had a break from one till two and another break at four, for a quarter of an hour.

There were three groups: Sister Theresa's, Sister Bernard's and Sister Paschal's. Each group had a dormitory with about forty or fifty people in it. The groups had their own TV room, and we all ate in the refectory, which was a big room. The refectory had square tables which sat about four people, and we got our dinner from the hot press. The dinner was all right: it must be hard to cook for a lot of people. We had stews, fish, vegetables, potatoes and meat, and for dessert, rice, semolina, sago or custard and apple. On different mornings for breakfast we had porridge, cornflakes, bread, tea and eggs. For tea we had bread, toast and beans and a fry.

I was in Lourdes with the women about five times. We went to help out with the sick. I was working in the laundry over there with the women. We got into the cold water in the baths. I went shopping for things like holy souvenirs. I went to the grotto, which was lovely and peaceful.

A teacher came to me on Fridays. The nun must have got her for me. I was the only one going to her; I was much younger than the other women. The teacher saw me for a few weeks. She was a very nice older woman. I did reading. When I was living with the women sometimes we would have a laugh if anything happened. I used to say, 'All the handies are all off.' Then if things were all right I would say, 'All the handies are all on.'

Some weekends I used to do the nuns' garden with some of the other women. A garden man came as well to do the garden. It was nice doing the garden and we had fun. One day when I was doing the garden I fell into the rose bushes and the women had a great laugh at the way I fell in; I was laughing as well. Some weekends I worked in the North Star Hotel, cleaning in the kitchen and washing up the pots.

We went to Skerries for holidays for two weeks. We had to split our two weeks: we had one week at the beginning of the summer and one at the end. About eight people went at a time. The nuns had a house down there. We had a beautiful holiday with the nuns. They gave us a good fry: eggs, sausages, rashers and black and white puddings. For dinner we had soup, fish, meat, vegetables and potatoes, and for dessert we had custard or rice most days. Tea was toast, eggs, a fry and scrambled eggs. The nuns did all the cooking. We had a good lie on in the mornings. We got out for walks at the beach and I would go sunbathing. We were allowed to do our own thing once we were back in time for dinner and tea. After breakfast, dinner and tea we all helped to clean up. The nuns would give us a hand and we would say to them, 'You shouldn't help with the washing up, you did the cooking.'

4
—

TRAINING

After being taught by the elderly teacher I was sent down
to the school in the convent in Rivilla. The school and the
hostel were for the young people; I was still living with
the elderly women. There were young people in the
school. We did reading, writing, sewing on the machine,
cookery, crafts, gymnastics, sums and singing. There was
a gymnastics teacher who called me into the room on my
own. I would not go in because he was a man. He was nice,
though. Another time, one of the girls threw my keys over
the wall. Maybe she was jealous. We did the same things
as in a normal school. One summer the weather was very
good. After school I went to the garden in the convent
with the girls and we sunbathed.

When I came back for tea the elderly women said,
'Where were you?' I said I had been in the sun. The women
said, 'You should have been working in the laundry after
school.' I didn't listen to them.

One day the teacher went out of the classroom and a
big black spider was on the floor coming towards me. I
got up on the table. The teacher came in and saw me

there. He said, 'You'd think an elephant was coming into the room.'

When we did sewing I used to go mad with the machine, and one of the girls, Patricia, would say to me, 'Come on and get your coat on and we'll bring the sewing machine to Grangegorman.' We had great fun. We used to have a fancy dress. I was a punk rocker and I did 'The Circus Came to Town' with a few girls. I won trophies for fancy dress, which we did in a big room in the elderly women's side.

When I finished in the school at the age of about eighteen, Sister Lucy got me into Rehab in Pleasant Street. I was a day pupil; I was still living with the elderly women in the convent in Sean McDermott Street. It was nice in the Rehab; I enjoyed the atmosphere. I did sewing there on the sewing machine. We had a teacher in once a week on a Friday for reading and writing. We had to bring in our lunch bread but we were given soup. We worked from nine o'clock until around five. We had a break from one till two and another at three, for fifteen minutes. But I was only there for a year and a half and then I had to leave. I wasn't told why I had to leave. I asked the nun whether I could change to the Rivilla hostel in the convent and she said I could.

The staff did our dinners when all the girls came back from work. When I was home, at around six o'clock, we had a nice dinner: vegetables, potatoes, meat, fish or stew most days. There were about ten girls there. We had a small dormitory: a room with curtains for a door. After I left the Rehab I got help from the nun to see whether I could get an outside job, but they said I was too slow.

The women in the laundry were helping me to try to get faster at doing the work.

5

MY WORKSHOP DAYS

So the nun, Sister Lucy, got me going to St Michael's House in Templeogue. I was still living in Sean McDermott Street in the Rivilla hostel. I was paying rent of £16 a week to the nun: when you are not working in the laundry you pay your keep, but if you work in the laundry you don't have to. One of the girls said to me, 'You're going to St Michael's because of your pimples.' I would scream at her and say, 'It's not because of my pimples.'

In the Michael's House workshop I used the sewing machine. The material I was sewing was woven by the other workers in the weaving room in the workshop. They weaved the material and rugs. It was grand; we had fun. Then there were cutbacks and the sewing was done away with. But I learnt a lot when I was there, like independence and cookery. We had a break from one o'clock till two and another at three for fifteen minutes. We had to bring in our own lunch: bread with cheese or meat. We had to put addresses on the envelopes and put things into envelopes. I didn't like that because there was no skill in it.

When I was in the hostel there was one time we all had

an outing and the elderly women came as well. We went to some hotel and had dinner and a disco. I had wine and one of the girls put more in my glass. I then got drunk with drink. I did not know what I was doing for the rest of that night. When I got home I remember when one of the girls was putting me to bed I said to her, 'I want to wash my teeth.' She said, 'Your teeth will be all right, just get to bed.' The next morning I had to go to work, but I felt like not going. The girl who had put me to bed said, 'You have to go to work.' I had a hangover. The people that were out with me were not pleased with me over what happened. We had cleaning jobs to do in the hostel. I had to do the toilets and I did my own washing.

One of the girls, Susan, brought me to see the film *The Exorcist*. It was about a girl who was possessed by the devil, so I was crying my head off. One of the girls gave me a cup of tea. That helped, and then I went to bed. But I was so frightened I could not stay in bed. I had to sleep with someone for a week. Another girl, Helen, brought me roller skating. We went roller skating most nights in Sean McDermott Street, which was just around the corner. It was a disco on skates. There were sometimes competitions. I won a free ticket to come again and another time there was a dress-up night. I dressed up as Charlie Chaplin and won a free ticket. I was good on the skates but not brilliant at it. I liked the disco, though.

One Halloween night we had a Halloween party and games like getting money and nuts in the basin of water. We had a competition of snap-the-apple. The apple was hanging from the ceiling and we had to keep our hands behind our backs. Susan and I were left in the finals of the competition of snap-the-apple, and I won: the prize was sweets. Then the next day Susan said I had bitten her lip. I did not know whether I had, but her lip was swollen.

I had pimples all over my face. In the hostel one of the girls used to say to me, 'You will never get them pimples away from your face.' I was very annoyed. I used to cry a lot because of the pimples. When I was at the prayer meeting I kept asking God to take the pimples off my face. I enjoyed the prayer meetings. We had them in Sean McDermott Street convent. We prayed and sang lovely songs about God. I enjoyed all the songs. I would love it if that girl could see me now because the pimples are gone from my face, thank God. He heard my prayers. God is slow but he does listen. Mrs Butler and Ann brought me out to Father Moore's Well. It helped get rid of my pimples.

In the workshop the workers had a big canteen with large round tables for break time. About eight people could sit around the tables and the staff had their own room for their break. One day a man called Julian came to see who would be interested in gymnastics. He was looking at us doing forward rolls to see who could do it. Then after a while I was picked to go to the gymnastics club on Thursday mornings. The manager in the work-shop let me go to gymnastics every Thursday morning for two hours; then I had to go back to the workshop. I had to get two buses. We had a gymnastics teacher called Mary Davis. She was a lovely teacher and she was funny. Then we had gymnastics on Tuesday night from about seven o'clock to about half past eight. I enjoyed going to gym-nastics. The club was in St Michael's House School in

Ballymun. I used to arrive for gymnastics early and go to the training centre in St Michael's House and play snooker. The training centre was near the school.

Then I was put on work experience. I worked in Quinnsworth. I was two weeks there. The girl who was showing me the work I had to do was very nice. I was packing shelves with biscuits, sweets and other types of food. I enjoyed it. When my work experience was finished, the workers gave me a lovely present. They signed their names on the card and I got a lovely big towel and a jumper.

We did an independence course in the workshop in Templeogue. We did cooking and shopping for food. We cooked vegetables, potatoes, meat, shepherd's pie, steak-and-kidney pie and flapjacks. We wrote down things that you need for cooking and in the kitchen, sitting room and all around the house.

We were taught everything you need to know about moving into a new place, including how to find out where the nearby places are. You would need to know where the doctor, church, supermarket, and gardaí and others are. If you had food left over, you had to put it in a Pyrex dish with cheese sauce and cook it afterwards. We learned about clothes, like following washing instructions and hand-washing clothes. The staff showed us a video of safety in the home and kitchen. In Dublin city centre we got a map of Dublin. The staff drew it out with the streets. We learned things about living on your own like bills, managing your money for the flat and emergencies. We went to the caravan park in Rosslare, County Wexford for a week. We went out for walks sometimes, to the beach and the pub, and we watched TV. We went shopping for food and did cleaning things. We cooked our own food and did the washing up and cleaning up after dinner. For dinner we would do fish, meat, vegetables, potatoes, shepherd's pie, steak-and-kidney pie and flapjack biscuits. For breakfast I had cornflakes. Some of the time we could do our own thing. We went on the train to Wexford and came back on it. There was a staff member with us. We learned these things in the workshop as well before we went to the caravan. The staff member had a training room in the workshop to train people to become independent. She brought us to Rosslare and Wexford and Kelly's Hotel. There were lots of things to do, like swimming, playing games, doing gym and dancing at nighttime. The food was lovely.

When I was in the workshop I went for some weekends to Rossmore Hostel in St Michael's House. The staff in the hostel asked me up. I enjoyed the hostel: we all had a nice dinner together. That is how I heard about the hostel in St Michael's House. The social worker from St Michael's House was doing a waiting list for the hostel, so I got my name down on it. I was a good while waiting – around two years. I left Sean McDermott Street and stayed at home.

*

At night at home I would have my dinner. Then after dinner I went out with the children to play football, chasing and running on the tarmacadam playground in St Martin's Avenue. We had great fun. Some nights I would stay in watching TV.

My sister Cathy was born in Holles Street Hospital. When I was sixteen, a few years after the birth of Cathy, we moved to St Martin's Avenue. I have five brothers and three sisters and there were four other children who died young in the family. Four brothers are married, and so are three sisters, and one brother is single and living at home. My eldest sister, Mag, and her husband, Christy, have nine children: three are married, some are working, and the rest are at school. My brother John Joe and his wife, Brigid, have one child, who is at school.

6

GOING TO LOURDES

My brother Jimmy and his wife, Marion, have had three
children. One is at school, the other goes to a workshop
in Kare, and the third died of spina bifida when he was
five. Before he died people in Naas raised money for him
and a group of people with disabilities to go to Lourdes.
I was one of the people who went, with Marion and her
child. It was my second time in Lourdes and we stayed
in a hotel. The food was not nice there. It was not like
our own food. I had to take the child's Liga all the time.

We went to the grotto. It is lovely and peaceful. There
were nice shops with holy things. I bought some souvenirs
of Lourdes. One of the girls in the group annoyed me
about my pimples coming and going. I went to the grotto
on my own and to the baths in Lourdes. I prayed to God
for the pimples to clear. When you get out of the baths
you are almost dry and you get dressed. One night there
was thunder and lightning. Marion was telling me about
it. She was trying to wake me up but I would not wake
up. She said I kept snoring all the time and she could not
go to sleep. She was telling me all the others in the group

went downstairs in the hotel because they were afraid of the thunder and were going to go home, but they didn't.

One day a group of us were going to Mass. We had to go down a big hill and I asked could I push the boy in the wheelchair. I was wheeling the boy and on the way down he fell out of the wheelchair. Then I was crying all the time but his mother said he would be all right. So we went to Mass and I was still crying; I cried through the whole of the Mass. When we came out of Mass the boy's mother said he was all right, so I stopped crying.

My brother Martin and his wife, Ann, have five children, including four boys; all but one of their children go to school. My brother Thomas and his wife, Susan, have one girl, who does not go to school yet. My sister Cathy and her husband, Tony, have three boys; two of them go to school. My brother Nicholas lives at home. My sister Mary and her husband, Michael, have one girl, who goes to school. They lived in Athlone for about four years and then emigrated to Australia. They have been there for about ten years and she is enjoying living over there. The rest of my sisters and brothers live in Naas. I wonder how my family put up with me when I was young; but my family love me and they are good to me, and I get on well with them.

When I was at home I had to get the eight o'clock country bus to Dublin, and then I had to get another bus in Dublin. I went up to Sean McDermott Street for the weekends to a casual unit in the same convent.

There were six girls there and we shared bedrooms. My bedroom had a door like a house. There was one girl, Patricia, in the hostel who I got friendly with. She was sharing the bedroom with me at weekends and she was very nice. She had dark hair and was about the same size as me. One night I was doing my sewing, with a Celtic pattern, and one of the girls kept cutting my thread. My friend Patricia gave out to her. There was another time Patricia had a lovely pair of white trousers and she cut them too short and the same girl that cut my thread would not stop laughing. Patricia was annoyed about this. I said to her, 'Oh, I have a very good idea. Give me them and I will make them into pedal-pushers.' Patricia thought I would fix them for her. We had a great laugh afterwards.

Sister Lucy used to come over to the hostel, and sometimes she would watch TV with us. Helen or other girls did the cooking for us. It was nice. There was a sitting room, a dining room, a kitchen and a nice garden out the front.

7

HOSTEL GROUP HOME

Finally, I got word to go to St Michael's House, a hostel on Kennington Road in Templeogue. My family brought me up to Dublin with my things and we had tea and cake. My family talked to the staff. It was a semi-independent house – like a normal house in the community. I lived there for six years. There were staff there all the time, and one staff member slept overnight in their own bedroom. The other staff who were working would come in and out and talk to the head staff in the house. The staff worked different days and nights. In the house there was a bathroom and toilet, four bedrooms upstairs and one downstairs, which was a converted garage. I was sharing the bedroom with another woman. There was a sitting room, a dining room, a kitchen and a nice garden front and back.

When we cooked the staff were there if we needed a hand. I learned a lot, like cooking and doing my clothes, and I got a lot faster at doing things. After dinner we took turns to do the washing up and to clean up the kitchen. I would cook potatoes, vegetables, meat, shepherd's pie, chicken casserole, roast chicken and roast potatoes. Sometimes we would have dessert, like custard, rice, or ice cream. In the mornings I would have cornflakes. We would have dinner around six o'clock. We had duties to do before we went to work. My duty was the bathroom and toilet. I learned about independence. It was a mixed hostel, with three women and two men. We had our own keys to get in and out. We had Christmas parties in the house and we had our friends and families to the party.

We had good fun getting the food ready, like the drinks, cake, Tayto and peanuts. It was a good night. We would talk and have records on and some people would do disco dancing. Then another time we would have a night out for Christmas. We would have a Christmas dinner and then go to the cabaret. We had music and we would dance. Then we had a break from dancing and people would do things like singing, telling jokes and dancing. When the people were finished with the acts we would have dancing again until about one o'clock in the morning. Then we would go home to bed. Then we had another night to ourselves with the staff giving out our Christmas presents. It was great fun giving the presents. Sometimes the staff brought us to the pub, and sometimes we went on our own in a group. The head of staff, Sheila, left to go to Florida in America. We gave her a going-away present. I was sorry to see her go. Then we got a new head of staff. She was very nice.

8

MY TRIP TO FLORIDA

A year later I and one of the women went to America to
see Sheila. She met us at the airport. It was lovely and
sunny all the time. I was raging about my clothes on the
first day of my holiday. All our luggage went astray at
the airport and we had nothing to wear. Sheila had to give
us clothes to wear because we had winter clothes on us –
all our summer clothes were in our cases. She brought
us to the beach the first day. We got our cases the next
day. I was happy to have my own clothes. The beach was
near us up the road. The women and myself were at the
beach all the time. I went to the beach two days on my
own because the other woman was sick. Sheila brought
us out to Waterworld. These were lots of things there, like
slides down into the water and water tubes. I was on the
tube all the time and enjoyed myself. Later on, we had to
go into the shop to shelter from thunder and lightning.
We were frightened.

Sheila brought us to see Disneyland another day. We
went to see the Disney characters. We went on a boat
underwater and went on some of the amusements. I

enjoyed looking at the small lizards: they go really fast. I had pizza to eat all the time; I loved the pizza over there. I had cornflakes in the mornings. We were there for two weeks with Sheila and her boyfriend. He was very nice. They have a nice house. The last day when we went back to the airport it was lashing rain: we had been very lucky with the weather for our holidays.

9

MY SPORT

I was in Kennington Road when I was doing the Special Olympics. I was training a lot for them. I went to the gymnastics club twice a week. I used to do gymnastics in the dinner room when there was no one there.

I did a lot of competitions for the Special Olympics. I was in Gormanston for the weekend doing gymnastics and I won first prize. We slept in a boarding school in a big dormitory in bedrooms with doors. We had a good time and the food was nice. Then in Limerick there was a video programme of me made called *Let Me Win*. It was fun getting on TV – I enjoyed it. I won first prize for gymnastics and second for running. When I had finished the gymnastics competition and got the medal I could not get dressed with people and my family coming over to me; they were all pleased with me. It was a good weekend. I went to Brussels in Belgium twice for the Special Olympics for gymnastics. I won first and second prizes.

At the European Games I won three gold medals and two silver medals for gymnastics. The Games were in UCD in Dublin. I learned a lot in the Special Olympics about travelling, going out and meeting friends at the competitions. I had to remember my sequence when I was doing it and had to keep in rhythm with the music. After the European games my family had a party for me in St Martin's Avenue in Naas in the tarmacadam playground. They had music and bunting up and flags saying 'Good Luck'. We had cakes, sweets and things like that. I had a great time. My neighbours in St Martin's gave me money. I was picked for America for the World Special Olympics Games along with two boys from St Michael's House Ballymun Gymnastics Club. We did a lot of training; it was hard work. Then the gymnastics club got us going to Bayside Gymnastics Club because they have bars. In St Michael's House Gymnastics Club there were only mats for the floor, a beam and a vault. Bayside Gymnastics Club had more equipment.

We also had lots of weekends doing gymnastics training for America. When I was in America I was in an act for the opening ceremony of the Olympics on the stage. The act was about doing gymnastics. The music was called 'I'm So Excited'. The group of us doing the act all had learning difficulties. In America I did a lot of training for it. Then a few days later it was shown on American TV. We went to the pub to see it. The opening ceremony and all the other acts were shown on the TV except our act. I was very unhappy because I would have loved it to have been on TV.

For the gymnastics competitions I was on the floor, beams, bars and vault. I enjoyed it. I won two gold and three silver medals. I didn't like the food, though: there were times when I couldn't wait to get home for my food in Ireland.

We had a great welcome at Shannon Airport. People

were singing and the media were there. I was on the news showing my medals. The man from Kare brought two of us back to Kennington Road. Another girl who was in America was also from Naas. Her name is Fidelma and she was doing bowling. When we came back to Kennington Road the staff had cake and sandwiches ready. The staff were saying to me, 'You have to go home', but I was saying that I wasn't going home for a few days. But the staff still said, 'You have to go home.' They knew that there was something prepared at home but I did not know what it was – the staff would not tell me anything.

I had to get ready and the men from Kare brought the girl and me down to Naas. When we got to Naas there was a big float to bring us into the town. The people in Naas had it all arranged. When we got to the town hall in Naas, Fidelma and I were given a bouquet of flowers and a certificate for the Special Olympics. A speech was made and photos were taken of us with our families. Then when it was finished my friends and family told me to wait with the man from Kare for a while. The he brought me to my house in St Martin's Avenue. My family had a big party prepared for me.

As soon as I got out of the van, the children got me up dancing. There were flags saying 'Good Luck' and pictures up all over the house. After a good while a van with hot dogs and chips came to the street. My mammy was saying it would be good if the media were there. The party was outside the front of the house. Then when it all died down I asked mammy could I lie down for a while before the other party. So after my lie down I got ready to go to Fidelma's party.

My mother and I were invited to that party. When I got there I was talking and saying hello to people. Then I was dancing all the time outdoors until my mother came for me and I had to go home. My brother Martin took a video of the three parties, which were one after the other on the same day. I was so tired after it all I spent the whole of the next day in bed.

The following day Fidelma and I and our parents were asked down to the ESB office in Naas, where we were presented with a microwave oven. We got our photos taken for the *Leinster Leader*. When I had finished the competitions after America, I left the workshop.

*

For a good while I did not do gymnastics and was not involved with any gymnastics club. Then one day I went down to see the people at Bayside Gymnastics Club. Then Marie asked me whether I would like to help at the club. I said I would, and I have been helping at the club for about ten years.

I help with the special-needs group. I help to get them ready for the Gymnastics Fest for the Special Olympics and some of them go into the competitions for the Special Olympics. The Gymnastics Fest is a brilliant way of showing off their talents.

This is Bayside gymnastics club.

-coach

Jean

She doing the hand-stand on the bar

Now a coach in the gym club.

coach

Vault

This is the floor   Bridge

coach

Hand-stand

This is the coach

Oop hunted-cartwheel

walk over

PART II

10

GOING TO AUSTRALIA

I went to Australia to see my sister Mary on my own. The staff helped me to arrange the tickets, brought me to the airport and stayed with me until the plane was about to leave. Then I was on my own. I had help if I needed it from the air hostesses on the plane. The plane stopped in five places. Then my sister Mary, her husband, Mike, and their daughter Sylvia met me at the airport in Melbourne. It was a long drive to Stawell, Victoria. They were saying in the van that I must be tired. I said I was not tired, then I went dopey. They kept slagging me about that. When I got to their house I went to bed.

The next day I put away my clothes and settled into the bedroom. Mary took a few days off work to help me get to know my way around and find out where things were. When it was sunny I was in the garden all the time. When I had got used to the house Mary left me on my own until she got her summer holidays. She brought me to her job and I saw the sewing machines. It was all decorated for Christmas and looked lovely. It was a big factory. When Mary went on her month's holidays she brought me shopping to get presents and things like that. We went shopping for food for her house. Mary brought me on picnics to the lake. Most days we went sunbathing.

We also went on an outing to the gold mines. We played bowls and walked around looking for gold. You get a strainer and put it in the stream and look to see if there is any gold in it. We weren't lucky. Some days we went to the swimming pool in Stawell. It was not far from the house. We had barbecues all the time. They have a lot of barbecues in Australia and invite their friends to them. Sometimes I would sunbathe on my own and sometimes we would sunbathe together in the garden. Other times I played with Sylvia. I had lovely food because Mary cooks nice dinners all the time. On Christmas morning we went to Mass. We gave out our Christmas presents. I got a jumper. We all went to see the kangaroos and we saw some koala bears too. We had Christmas dinner in the house. One weekend we went camping with Mary's friends to the beach, where it was lovely for sunbathing.

One day it rained. I woke up and my bed was wet. I told Mary and she thought that I had wet it. I said I hadn't. They she saw it was the rain because the camp was wet. The day it was raining we played cards and had nice food. I did not like it when I got bites from mosquitoes. The crickets and mosquitoes come out when the sun has gone in. We went fishing for yabbies and then we cleaned and boiled them for tea or dinner. They were lovely.

My sister Mary brought me to a Christmas party where she works. It was a good night: we had dinner and then we had dancing with Mary and Mike. Another day Mary brought me to the park. Sylvia and I went on the swings and the other things in the playground. For breakfast I had cornflakes. Dinner was meat, vegetables and potatoes. I was there for ten weeks.

I did cleaning and ironing for Mary. Then when I was going home Mary, Mike and Sylvia came to the airport with me and waited with me until my plane left. Then my family and the staff came to meet me at Dublin Airport, and when I got home I went to bed because of the jet lag.

11

URSULA

One of the women left Kennington Road and went for a two-week trial to another house. Her name is Ursula. I knew her because she did gymnastics with me. Then a few weeks later, we heard she would be coming back to live in Kennington Road. Another girl and I went to Ballymun, where Ursula lived, to give her a hand with bringing things from home with her. When we were going back she had a big teddy and elephant and other things. I was carrying the big teddy. When we saw the bus, I had to run for it. I was running across the road and took a dive onto the road, and when I caught the bus some people were laughing at what happened. Ursula was laughing and I laughed too. Then we went to McDonald's and I got a milk shake. When we went home to Kennington Road we were still laughing at what had happened. Ursula was funny. We had fun listening to the tapes in the dinner room.

I had a great laugh with Ursula about independence because she knew the staff were helping me to become more independent. When Ursula heard the word independence on the TV or radio she would laugh with me.

I had a meeting with the staff and other people in the service. It was a meeting to talk about independence because I wanted to move out. At the meeting it was decided to do some weekends in Aylesbury Lawn House, which belonged to St Michael's House.

I had to get my food shopping and cleaning things for the weekends. I did my own cooking and looked after myself. I was in the house all on my own. I watched TV and did things you have to do and the staff saw I was doing very well. After a good few weeks I had another meeting with the staff and the people in the service. I asked at the meeting about Artane Hostel because I had heard it was an independent house – that means that there are not staff in the house all the time.

So I said that, before going to a flat, I would like to go to Artane. They all agreed with me but there was no room at that time, so the service got the garage made into a bedroom. I did not know they were doing it and so I was a good while waiting. The staff in Artane had to ask the people in the house if they were happy to have me living there. The people in Artane agreed. One day I came home from work and the head of staff told me, 'I've got news for you. You have been picked to go to Artane.' I jumped up and down when I heard that. I jumped up on the head of staff and nearly knocked the glasses off her face when she told me the news. When it happened about her glasses I said I was sorry and that I was excited about the news. Then she helped me move my things to Artane when I had all of them ready. Then one night the staff and the others from Kennington Road brought me out and gave me a nice present. I had asked for a money-box, and

I got it, as well as flowers and a card. They brought me out to dinner. The dinner was nice and I enjoyed the night. This is where my new life started. It is a normal house in Artane in the community. It was a mixed house, with three women and two men. Downstairs there was a kitchen, a sitting room, a garage that had been made into a bedroom – where I was sleeping – a toilet and a shower room, and upstairs there were four bedrooms, a bathroom and toilet and a dining room.

We would do our own cooking. I would cook a vegetable dish, shepherd's pie and vegetables, chicken casserole, potatoes, fish or meat. I had cornflakes in the mornings, and we had dinner about six o'clock. We took turns doing the washing and drying after dinner and cleaning the kitchen. We had good laughs. The staff would come in three times a week to see how we were doing and to look at the bills. They came in for just a few hours. We would go out for our birthdays in a group for dinners, plays and films, and every summer we went away for a long weekend to a hotel.

One year we went to Kelly's Hotel in Wexford. There was a lot to do, like swimming, crazy golf, draughts, gym and entertainment. We went dancing in the hotel at night-time. When the tango music came on I would say, 'Come on, we will do the tango.' We had fun. The food was lovely, especially the dinners.

12

MY SECOND TIME 'DOWN UNDER'

The second time I went to Australia I booked the tickets on my own. I was working in the Gresham Hotel then. I asked the staff to come to the airport to keep me company. When I was getting on the aeroplane the staff got in until I was leaving. The people on the plane looked after me if I needed help or if I needed to know things. Then my sister Mary, Mike and Sylvia met me at the airport in Melbourne. It was a long drive to Stawell again. I went to bed when I got to their house. Mary took one or two days off until I settled in. The house had been done up since I was there before: there was a new kitchen, a snooker table and a small swimming pool in the garden. I went sunbathing in the garden; that was lovely. I played with Sylvia in the swimming pool. I did some cleaning in the house and ironing for Mary. This time we had breakfast with her friends on Christmas morning.

We went to Mass, then opened our Christmas presents. I got a big swimming towel and a koala bear. We had Christmas dinner outside in the garden. Mary let me stay in the sun after dinner while she cleaned up. Then when she had finished cleaning up she came out into the sun. We all sunbathed and played in the swimming pool. Mary brought us to a koala-bear shop that was in the shape of a koala bear, and we went walking.

Then Mary asked me what I would like for my birthday. I said, 'Can I go to the beach?' So we went to the beach. It was a six-hour drive. We went to a caravan for about two weeks in Adelaide. I was at the swimming pool all the time. Some days Mary, Mike and Sylvia and I went to the beach. I made a birthday cake with the sand and the shells. We had fun sometimes playing cards with Sylvia. We went to friends of Mary's in Adelaide for dinner – it was a barbecue. We had a great day there. They were surprised how brown I was.

One day Mary, Mike, Sylvia and I went to the film *The Addams Family.* It was very good. I enjoyed the way the hand moved in the film: it ran along the floor by itself. Another day we went to a sing-song outdoors. There were people playing in the park and it was very different from Ireland because they were sitting at it as though they were watching a film. They do not dance like over here in Ireland. I was mad to dance. I was sitting for a good while, then finally I got someone to dance with me and some more people joined me; then it was great. Afterwards we came back to the house in Stawell.

I had a few days of my holidays left. People in Stawell said we were lucky we went to the beach because it had been raining all the time. On my last few days it was cold and raining. I had to wear winter clothes. We went fishing for yabbies. Mary, Mike, Sylvia, their friends and I played snooker all night as a group. We had great fun. Then one night we went out for dinner. It was a good night. Then when I was going home Mary, Mike, and Sylvia came to the airport with me until the aeroplane was about to leave. I had been in Australia for a month.

13

OUR NEW KITCHEN

In Artane we got a new kitchen done. We had great fun
in it. We had to eat in the sitting room while the kitchen
was being put in. Everything was cluttered together.
Sometimes we had to eat out when it became very dusty
inside because of the work being done on the kitchen.
When the kitchen was finished it was great and everything
was put back in the presses. The kitchen was lovely.

When you live in a hostel it is not easy because people
have different ways of living. Also, when you live in a
hostel you see your family's and friends' houses and you
wish you were them. I go home to my family the odd
weekend. I do not go home much because I am busy doing
things in Dublin. My family understands. I am busy with
meetings, going out to keep in touch with my friends
and doing things for myself. I need to do housework,
shopping and things like that. I have a good few friends.
I enjoy life. Sometimes I might go to films in town or
meet some friends for tea. I would go up to their houses
or sometimes they might come down to my place if they
are not busy. My two friends from Sean McDermott

Street are still friendly with me.

Sometimes my mother rings me. I could be out and my mother would say to me, 'You would need a rope to keep Rita in.'

14

——

BEING IN HOSPITAL

I was in the Mater Hospital for a big operation on my
ovaries. I had a big cyst on them. I was very nervous going
into hospital. After the operation I had to stay in bed for
a day or two. The doctor said after a day or two to walk
up and down the corridor; then when I had finished
walking along the corridor I would sit down on my bed. I
had great fun with the patients in my ward in the hospital.
Another time we had fun with the pillows I used during
the day. I would leave my pillows on the chair at night
because I do not use pillows at night, so the nurse took
them away. I was looking for them. Afterwards I got the
pillows back.

I said to the patient next to me, 'I know what I can do,
I will hide the pillows in the wardrobe so the nurse will
not get them.' That way I held onto my pillows. It was
great fun when my visitors came up to see me. One night
one of my friends, Niamh, was visiting me in hospital. She
asked me what would I like. I said I didn't want anything
and that I was all right, but she kept asking me what
would I like. So in the end I asked her for three night-

Rita's parents, Johnny and Kathleen

Rita (second from left) making her First Communion, with her
parents and sister Mary and brother Martin

Rita (front centre) with other residents
of St Theresa's in Blackrock

With the cast of *Glenroe*

On a Bayside Gymnastics Club trip with
club members Jessica (left) and Feargal

At the 1985 European Games,
held at the RDS, Dublin

Coaching a member of Bayside Gymastics Club

With boxer Muhammad Ali in Chicago in 1998 at an event to celebrate the thirtieth anniversary of the Special Olympics

With President Bill Clinton
at a dinner given at the White House
for Special Olympics athlethes, 17 December 1998

Later that evening, with other Special Olympics athletes,
President Clinton and First Lady Hillary Clinton

With members of the Irish team at the 1999 Special
Olympics World Games in North Carolina

With Special Olympics Chief Executive Tim Shriver (left)
and singer Stevie Wonder (centre) at the
1999 Special Olympics World Games

dresses. The next day Niamh came in with three night-dresses. So I thanked her. That night when Niamh had gone, my family came into the hospital to see me. I told them about Niamh and the three nightdresses and I showed them to my family. They got a great laugh out of it. I was two weeks in hospital. We watched Mass on the TV every morning before breakfast. The food in the hospital was lovely. We stayed in the new part of the hospital, which was like a hotel.

Artane House is an independent group home hostel. I learned a lot more about independence because I used to be on my own there without any of the staff. I spent between five and six years there. I enjoyed going out with my friends and doing my own things. I watched TV and did things like that. We had a nice garden front and back.

15

CHANGING MY JOB

After the competition in the Special Olympics I went to the workshop. They were all pleased in the workshop with how well I had done in the competitions. So it was a good few weeks after the competition that I asked to leave the workshop. This is where they started to teach me about work. I had a meeting with the staff and management in the workshop because I wanted to go to the Rehab in Ballyfermot. I did sewing on the machines. I was under terrible pressure. I could not stand ribbing. I had a lot of back trouble. I would prefer part-time work. I liked playing games on the computer. Sometimes I would read and write. The teacher came in on Friday. We started at nine o'clock. We had breaks from one to one thirty and for a quarter of an hour at three o'clock. We had to bring in our own lunch. We had bread, cheese or meat.

I got to know a girl called Jennifer, and I sat with her all the time. She was very nice and she worked on the sewing machine as well when there was no other work to be done. I became very friendly with her. We had fun in the Rehab together. Sometimes I met her for tea and we went for a look around the shops. She would ask me up to her place; she cooks lovely dinners – vegetable dishes, fish, potatoes and meat. Jennifer and I did not like the Rehab because the atmosphere was not nice, especially at the sewing machines. When there was nobody working at the machines we used to throw empty spools backwards and forwards to each other, and the staff would tell us to stop. I was about a year there and I am still good friends with her.

Then I told them in St Michael's House that I wanted to leave Rehab because I was not happy working in the workshop. I know that some people like working there but it wasn't for me. So then I was put into the St Michael's House Northbrook workshop. In the workshop I put light bulbs into blister packaging. The work was for shops. I did not enjoy it because I had to do the same thing over and over again. I do not like working with too many people. I was a good few weeks in the Northbrook workshop. When I went to the workshop I was told I would be about two weeks in it and that then I would get another job, but that did not happen, so I decided to walk out. If I had not walked out, I would probably still be there now, so I was happy when I did it. This is how I got to where I am today. I was told by the doctor if I did not get a job by the end of the year I would have to go back to the workshop.

Then I got help to go to work in the Ballymun Clinic in St Michael's House. I was working there for a while. The management and the people there were very nice. I did cleaning, hoovering, dusting, emptying the bins and sometimes photocopying. I worked a few hours a day and was off at weekends. Then in 1990 I got on a Cert course for ten weeks. The supervisor was very nice. It was hard to do the writing and get everything down. I got people on the course to help me write things down.

The girls thought the supervisor was helping me to get a job, but work experience was part of the course. I was a week in the Gresham Hotel for work experience. I got a certificate as a certified hotel assistant for the course when it was finished. Then I was out of work for a while after the course. In 1990 I refused to go back to any of the workshops. I know some people like the workshops, though.

I still go to see the people in Templogue workshop. I go in particular to say hello to the sewing teacher. They let me use the machine if I need to do any sewing on my clothes. I would be there all day because of the amount of sewing that I did, and I would also see them at break time. I enjoyed seeing them. There is usually a Christmas dinner every year and I am usually asked to go to it. I enjoy the dinner dance. We have lovely food there, like chicken, ham, vegetables, potatoes or chips, and for dessert we have ice cream and then tea. After the dinner we have a disco, which is very good. It is held in Jury's Hotel. There are usually spot prizes, and we also have a raffle ticket pinned to our clothes. Then if our number comes up we win a spot prize.

After about three months, I got lucky: I got word from the Gresham to come for a job. I have been there for nine years now on support placements. I work on a part-time basis, for four hours a day. I work four days one week and three the next.

I clean the lobby: I hoover, dust and clean the walls, toilets and workers' toilets. The people are nice – I have a good laugh with them. I am only allowed to earn so much money because of my Disabled Person's Maintenance Allowance (DPMA), even though my income is small. People with disabilities are only allowed to work so many hours part-time if they want to keep their DPMA. If you earn too much, benefits like the bus pass, medical card and living-alone allowance are taken away from you and it is very hard to get back on the DPMA money. It suits me because I will never work full-time, but there are people with disabilities who would like to work full-time and feel they can't.

When I first started in the Gresham there was one day when I went up to the first floor looking for cleaning things and got locked into the cupboard room on the first floor. To begin with I kept banging the trolley into the door, but then I finally thought of an idea. I got the badge off my uniform and stuck the pin into a bit of paper that I found. I wrote on it, 'Please help me' by making holes in the paper. Then I pushed it out through the door, but I kept banging the trolley against the door. One of the girls heard me. She was surprised at the way I had written the note and the way I shoved it out through the door. She brought me up to the supervisor. The supervisor asked me, 'How long were you in there for?' I said about three hours. I was very upset because I had got no work done. She said that it was all right. I was a while with the supervisor. Then she got me a taxi to take me home. She was a lovely supervisor. Afterwards I found out that I had got mixed up about which way to open the door. That supervisor is not in the hotel any more.

When I am cleaning the lifts some of the customers say to me, 'Will you clean my shoes too?' I have a good laugh with the customers and sometimes they tell me that they'd like to bring me home to clean their houses. I used to say to one of porters, 'Look into my eyes.' I love when I get him going because he is really funny, but I don't do it now.

We should be called people with
learning difficuilities or people with
learning disabilities

This is a
person
with learning
difficuilities
living on there
own going into
her House

Radio   RT.E.

going into
there
work.

16

MAKING THE PUBLIC MORE AWARE
OF WHAT'S IN A NAME

I am writing this to tell you about the expression 'mentally handicapped', which the services, parents and media use. What image does this give? I feel the services have an image problem. Services in other countries say 'people with learning difficulties' or 'people with disabilities' and make the image of their service clear. When we use the words 'mentally handicapped' it is not clear what the services are and who is being talked about. When you say 'mentally handicapped children' this does not mean me. Do I seem like someone who is 'mentally handicapped'?

I was not well one day. I was so sick I was barely able to walk. I wanted to go to the doctor, so I rang for a taxi and they asked for my address. I told them it was St Michael's House Hostel, Kennington Road, Templeogue, and then they asked me whether there was a staff member there. I said there wasn't, so they did not come for me: I had to walk to get the bus to go to the doctor.

One day I went to the swimming club and they asked me whether I could swim. I told them I could swim and had swum in the Special Olympics. They asked me where I lived. I told them that I lived in St Michael's Hostel, Kennington Road, Templeogue. They asked me whether there was a staff member with me. When I said there wasn't they would not let me swim.

These two stories show you that people do not understand the expression 'mentally handicappped', which the services use. It should describe who it serves and what it does in a positive way. Parents do not describe their children in a bad way. They would put a bad image on the child by calling him or her 'mentally handicapped'.

The service I am part of has done a lot of good for me and my friends. It has helped by bringing out the best in me. Because I was capable of cooking, it helped me to cook. Because I could live independently, it helped me to find and live in a flat. The service helped to bring out the potential I already had. But I still had to fight for this independence, and I have good support and friends. But the trouble is that any services that use labels like 'mentally handicapped' don't show that they know about people's potential. St Michael's House, though, doesn't use the expression 'mentally handicapped' any more but instead talks about people with learning difficulties.

People who run the service should be concerned about people with learning difficulties appearing in the media and speaking out. The services should be better for people with learning difficulties. These people can speak up for themselves just like other people.

We can eat, drink and go to the toilet just the same as you. We are just people with learning difficulties and disabilities. We are not 'mentally handicapped' or 'handicapped'. People of the younger generation need to be taught this by seeing people like us shown in the media in the proper way, like others are.

PARENTS

When I was at home on holidays from school my mother was afraid to let me at the cooker or to let me go to places on my own. But that is no problem any more. She has learned that I am grown up and can do things for myself. She does not have to worry about me and it makes her life easier and better. She is pleased for me. We have a good and normal relationship.

Parents should encourage their children when they are small to become independent and do things for themselves like going on the bus, doing housework, cooking, socialising, making friends and looking after their bodies. It is too late to do this when the parents are old and the children are grown up.

Parents often worry about what will happen to their children when they die. Parents can be overprotective and they shouldn't stop their children with learning difficulties from doing things for themselves. They should also help these children speak up for themselves.

SERVICES

People from the services would sometimes get someone with learning dificulties and disabilities on the media who could not speak up. People with learning difficulties and disabilities should be taught to speak up for themselves and should not be afraid. I would encourage people with learning difficulties to set up self-advocacy groups and get advice from outside the services. I would like to make a video, but I would need the money to make it and I would pick who should be in it.

labelling

Mentally handicapped =

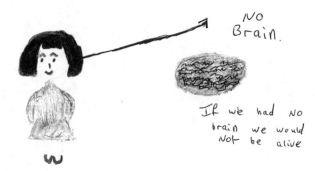

NO
Brain.

If we had NO
brain we would
Not be alive

can't do things
Just siting
there.

Mental Hospital

People
going
into Hospital

PART III

17

SELF-ADVOCACY

I was on the *Not So Different* radio programme for disabled people in 1990. Around that time I heard about the Forum of People with Disabilities, which was started in 1990. I got involved in going to their meetings when I heard about it. The forum does some self-advocacy work. Self-advocacy means standing up for yourself and your rights and not letting other people speak for you. You have to keep pushing and working hard and making sure people hear you and listen to you. The forum became a company in 1993 and has its annual general meeting each spring.

A group of us got together and talked about self-advocacy after the forum meeting was over, and we decided to set up our own group, the Dublin Self-Advocacy Group, which we founded in 1990. We meet once a month at the Welcome Inn.

Since I have been in self-advocacy groups like the Forum of People with Disabilities and the Dublin Self-Advocacy Group for people with learning difficulties, I have learned to speak up for myself. I now have the courage to go out and speak to the public and make my voice heard for the rights of people with disabilities. The groups help me a lot, for example with all the writing I have done as its secretary.

There are a few self-advocacy groups around Ireland for people with disabilities who are working hard for their rights. If you want to set up a self-advocacy group, you need to think about how many people would like to speak up for themselves. You will need a worker such as a secretary or advisor to be paid. You need to consider how this worker will be paid, who you will go to and write to, who will be the chairperson, who will be the treasurer, what will be on the agenda, what sort of things you will talk about, where the meetings will be held and whether you will meet once a week, once a fortnight or once a month. You also need to think about how long the meetings will last and whether you need transport.

When I was in the Dublin Self-Advocacy Group we talked about our advisors and what we wanted from them. This is a list that we discussed. Each member of the group was asked what they thought the role of the advisor was:

- Listen to what the group says, don't overpower it. Give the group help to speak up for themselves.

- Help with speech or writing. Give people a voice.

- Sit there as an equal (not as a staff member) and take things in. Help people say what they feel.

- Look at how to involve new members.

- Support people but don't make decisions for them.

- Be a point of contact between the Forum of People with Disabilities and people with learning difficulties.

People with learning difficulties are afraid to speak for themselves. Some people with learning difficulties do speak up, but I'd like to see more doing it. Don't be afraid to speak up, and tell people not to be afraid to speak up.

Speaking for Ourselves

We are speaking for ourselves
Speaking for ourselves
No one else can speak as well
Speaking for ourselves

Once I was afraid to speak
I was lonely I was weak
With a voice so very small
That I had no voice at all

Then I found a friend like me
And another made us three
And we laughed and then we cried
And then this is what we tried

We've been called by many names
We've been made to feel ashamed
We've been locked behind a door
But we'll come outside once more

by Karl Williams

*

A few years ago I did a course in public speaking with Carr Communications. This has given me the opportunity to speak in public about various subjects, including women's rights and people with disabilities. I have been interviewed on various television and radio programmes, including *Teletalk, Checkup, Not So Different* and Pat Kenny's radio programme. I have also visited schools around the country to speak to parents and families of people with disabilities.

I appeared on the television programme *Get a Life* and talked about the work I do in the Gresham Hotel and how it gave me the courage to get out of the workshops.

My achievements over the years have been recognised with certificates and awards from People in Need, Naas Urban Council, St Michael's House and the Special Olympics, amongst others.

In September 1998 I was chosen by *Irish Tatler* magazine as one of the Top 100 women who changed the face of Ireland.

We have a chairperson
and 3 advisers.

I am the
secretary
of the
Group.

18

MY TRIP TO AMERICA

The Irish Women's Research Project on people with
disabilities was the reason I visited the United States. I
gained a lot of experience with the group, and the
American groups learned from us. Angela invited me to
her house because we were flying from Belfast that
morning. It was a lovely house. It was the first time I had
stayed with two people in wheelchairs; I saw that they can
do the same things as anybody else. She helped me with
my writing and spelling. She taught me about people in
wheelchairs and the problems they face, like steep hills
and kerbs. Wheelchairs need wide doors, wheel-in show-
ers, low light switches, and pipes that are covered to
prevent burns. I was surprised by the dropped curbs –
cuts on the paths for wheelchairs. When I got to America
I made friends with Carolyn. She is a black lady and was
an escort officer with our group. Black people are discriminated against in the same way that people with
disabilities are.

I also made friends with Ilona. She was also an escort
officer with our group. She helped me to take notes at

some of the meetings and we had laughs and fun in the free time. We talked a lot about ourselves and the trip. The group I was with were very nice and we have remained good friends. I was impressed with the wonderful dropped curbs on the paths for wheelchairs and the way the door opens when a wheelchair-user presses a button outside the building. I learned from this trip about cross-communication. I know about other disabilities and the other people in the group have learned about learning difficulties. I got ideas from the group for my writing. At the meeting I was surprised and impressed by how a job coach helps give people with learning difficulties confidence to do their work, even in an outside job.

I liked the dogs for people who are deaf. The dog gets the person out of bed when the alarm clock goes off; it also opens the door and gives the phone to the person when it rings. There was also a dog for a person in a wheelchair; the dog picks up things that fall on the floor.

Disabled people in America have the same problems as those in Ireland. People with AIDS are discriminated against just like people with other disabilities. One meeting I was at was the highlight of the trip. People with learning difficulties made things like Christmas cards, soft toys for Christmas trees, and Christmas decorations for a charity shop. I got great ideas from some people at the meeting – for example, how to make baskets with holly. The things they make for the shop would show that people with learning difficulties are talented. I hope people have the vision to see and feel that kind of thing.

We had a few free days to see the sights. We stopped at the White House and took photos and went on a history tour of Washington, D.C. We saw President Kennedy's grave, the Abraham Lincoln Memorial and many other interesting sights. We also had a meeting where we talked to people who had sustained disabilities through war. Everywhere we went we had meetings and talked about different issues, like Goodwill in America. The Goodwill Group showed drawings to help people decide what job to choose. They talked about the clothes they sell to people and the fact that they have to make sure that the clothes are right before selling them. They also talked about jobs for people with hearing disabilities. Some people with hearing disabilities have a job coach who helps them get jobs.

One of the meetings we had was with the National Council on Independent Living. Ann-Marie Haughney, the executive director, spoke to us about the history of the independent living movement, which started in Berkeley, California in the sixties. She spoke about her group, which is called NICE. We went for lunch and missed our next meeting at the Senate. We went to the post office instead and posted a box to Ireland of printed material: it cost us $29. Then after we were finished at the Post Office the rest of the day was free. We were at the hotel doing our own thing.

On Friday morning we had another plane ride, to Minneapolis. We met Andy Fuller there and talked about people with all sorts of disabilities. We saw a video at the centre about doing things like living outside and living in an institution. The centre was very good. Then we had a tour around the centre and saw the swimming pool that helps disabled swimmers; I had a swim in the pool. After my swim the centre and our group had a social over lunch. We went to Gateway Education centre and met Dr Dole and talked. Then after the talk we looked at the children's toys. The toys had switches for children who do not have much movement and drawings for children who cannot talk. They showed us pictures of a wheelchair which was specially designed to go to the beach.

We did a lot of sightseeing tours all over America; we went to Manhatten and the river waterfall at Missisippi. We also went to the Hall of America in Minneapolis. Carolyn brought me to the amusements, and we had good fun. I was very surprised that the mall and the amusements were all indoors – it was so big.

We met with the Arc organisation about the media. We talked about the media and how it reaches out to families of children with disabilities. Arc works with the media and the way in which people with disabilities are portrayed by them.

Then we took a flight to San Francisco. All the group went over the Golden Gate Bridge and stopped to take photos at the visitors point. After lunch we went to Muirwoods, where there were redwood trees, which are the biggest trees in California. The group visited the home of Theresa, who is from Greenboro, and we met her mother. They are very nice people. Theresa is a wheelchair-user. She does a lot of writing: she writes poems and short stories. Her mother showed us all around the house. It was lovely. There was a small room for a wheelchair. Theresa is severely disabled and depends on a respirator to breathe. In spite of this she teaches part-time.

We then flew to Greensboro, North Carolina. The group

asked for an extra meeting for the blind. We had a talk first, then a tour around the building. The training that they do is very good. I took a photo of the craftwork.

We were invited to meet the residents of Bell House Inc and share their evening meal. Bell House is a federal- and state-funded hostel designed for independent living for disabled people on low incomes. Some of the twenty-two residents work outside Bell House. Professional care is provided. I was surprised with the things they used for their dinner when they were eating: they used an eating tray to make themselves as independent as possible. We had a social with Mary Lee Bales and staff from Gateway.

Then I took some photos of the house. The way the food was done made me think of Australia. On our last night in America the others in the group went to a musical. I do not like that sort of thing. I did some writing and got my bags ready for coming home to Ireland.

In America I loved the chicken grills. I had them all the time. When I went off for lunch or dinner it was my favourite food. When you go out for dinner over there, it is much different than over here, because when you go out there you first of all wait for a good while when you have a drink, then you wait another good while and you get your food then. When you do get your dinner the plate is full up, as if you were eating for two people.

Carolyn and Ilona saw us off at the airport when we got our flight home. With all the flights we had it was tiring. I was glad to be back in Ireland.

19

MY DREAM COME TRUE

In 1991, while I was living in a hostel in Artane, I got the idea that I would like a place on my own. I wanted to enjoy doing my own thing in my own time. A scheme for the 'mentally handicapped' came up on the TV and radio. My mother said to get my name on the waiting list, so I did. After two years, my name was taken off the waiting list.

So, this is when it all happened. I wrote in to the TV and radio programmes. I wrote to the government and TDs. I wrote because I was angry; I did not want to spend the rest of my life in a hostel. I saw lots of people to try to get a place of my own. I wrote letters, made phone calls, went for interviews and sent in forms. Finally, my TD got me on the HAIL waiting list. HAIL, the Housing Association for Integrated Living, houses people. I was a good while waiting and then I got word to go for the interview. This was the time I was in America for the women's project for people with disabilities. When I came back from America I got the keys to my apartment.

I had to clean the presses after the builders in my new

place. I had to wait in Artane until the staff could help me move my things to the apartment. I had to keep going up and down to Artane and Edenmore. When they helped me move I sorted all my things out. Then when my wardrobe was moved we discovered that it was too big to fit through the door of my apartment. The staff had to dismantle the wardrobe in the hallway on the stairs. So then I had to stay in Artane until my brother Nicholas and my uncle could come and put my wardrobe back together again.

I also had no heat in the apartment, so I arranged for the gas people to come and fit a gas heater. I think that was the worst part of moving in. Then finally I moved in on 25 May 1995; this was my first night in my new home. The neighbours were very nice. It was hard to find time to do things when I was sorting the place out. It was good when I got everything arranged. My mother and brother helped me a lot. I am very happy in my new apartment. I really enjoyed my first Christmas in the apartment, putting up miniature Christmas decorations. Having a home of my own for the very first time in my life is something I thought would never happen. Now I am forty-one years old and I am an independent person and like to have time to myself. But at the same time I like company and it is wonderful to go out and meet friends and then know that I can come home to my own place.

I was at Jennifer's house one night when I saw this poem, which I really liked. I like the way it talks about having time for yourself and all the other things it says:

Take Time

Take time to think,
It is the source of power.
Take time to read,
It is the foundation of wisdom.

Take time to play,
It is the secret of staying young.
Take time to be quiet,
It is the opportunity to seek God.

Take time to be aware,
It is the opportunity to help others.
Take time to love and be loved,
It is God's greatest gift.

Take time to laugh,
It is the music of the soul.
Take time to be friendly,
It is the road to happiness.

Take time to dream,
It is what the future is made of.
Take time to pray,
It is the greatest power on earth.

There is time for everything.

by Karl Williams

INDEPENDENCE

HAIL tenants said that independence means having a home of your own, taking control of your own life and making decisions for yourself. HAIL believes housing projects like this are the way forward in ensuring that individuals with special needs, either physical or mental, are integrated back into the community and allowed live full and active lives. HAIL needs more funds to build more projects like the Edenmore development. This development, which includes ten family houses, five single-storey one-bedroom houses for wheelchair-users and eight personal apartments, provides much-needed rented social housing. One resident described getting a place in this development as being like winning the Lotto.

20

COUNTER BALANCE DANCE AND DISABLED

Counter Balance began after the visit of Cando Dance Co from London in 1994. They were brought over by the Dance Company of Ireland and the Dublin Theatre Festival. What this highlighted for us here in Ireland was both the artistic and physical nature of the work. Integrated dance challenges the stereotypes that we hold about what people with disabilities can do and about who should and shouldn't dance, so Very Special Arts, together with the Dance Company of Ireland, started to fund the development of an integrated group here in Dublin called Counter Balance. The group is made up of members of the Wide Dance Community, Cerebral Palsy (Ireland), St Michael's House and other such ventures.

The group met once a week for two hours. Counter Balance put on a performance in June 1996. We had very vigorous rehearsals over five or six weeks. We performed a piece called 'Over, Under, Round and Through' by Cathy O'Kennedy and Trish Glynn, choreographers who have been working with the group. Another of the pieces we put on, 'I Love You But Sometimes You Drive Me Mad', by Kevin Murphy, looks at conflict and caring.

I think that the work will speak for itself. The kind of dance technique that the choreographers used is about the nature of contact. The reason improvisation works so well is that people with disabilities tend to create very different shapes. One of its empowering elements is its challenge against stereotyping disability. This sort of dance allows for different forms of expression with vigorous and challenging movements.

21

CHANGES IN THE WORLD

Years ago things was great. People could leave their doors open and walk the streets and feel safe. Life wasn't a grab for money. In the world today times are very bad because of crime. Nobody is safe these days. People changed when crime got bad. Money is evil today. The Green Party spoke out about greed and waste years ago and people wouldn't listen. Now I think it's too late here. Still, in America things used to be very bad and now New York is said to be the safest large city in the world. They are practising zero tolerance. Maybe we should practise it here. If people don't listen to this, the next generation will have no chance and will be afraid to walk the streets. People are afraid to speak up for their rights; they are afraid of being picked on. People blame God for the way things are in the world, but it is not God's fault, it is the fault of people themselves. We are destroying the world with greed and crime.

I want to live in a world where I am called a person with a learning disability, not mentally handicapped.

I want to live in a world where a person with a disability can get married if they want to.

I want to live in a world where no one is frightened of being discriminated against or attacked.

I want to live in a world where people with disabilities can appear on TV – the most powerful medium of the modern world.

I want to live in a world where there is no violence and all human beings coexist peacefully.

I want to live in a world where we share in the light of God's glory through His Son, the Light of the World.

I want to live in a world where things are put right now, not in a few years' time, when we could be dead.

That's the kind of world I want to live in.

22

GLOBAL MESSENGER OF THE SPECIAL OLYMPICS

I started with the Special Olympics in 1978. Since then, the Special Olympics has opened up a whole new world for me. It has helped me to meet new people and trust them. It has helped me to travel on my own.

Gymnastics is my sport. I have learned a lot of gymnastic skills, and the greatest joy for me was to represent Ireland in the International Games in South Bend, USA in 1987. I went on to win the all-round competition.

Having the chance to compete in gymnastics has given me the courage and confidence to do my daily job. Now I am a gymnastics coach in Bayside. I have been able to share my joy and happiness with my friends and family. I have made them feel proud of me.

I have made true friends through the Special Olympics. One of them is Mary McEvoy, the actress from Glenroe. I have had special moments when all eyes were looking at me. It is thanks to the Special Olympics that I have had those special moments.

1998 is the thirtieth anniversary of the Special Olympics. To help celebrate, twelve athletes from around

around the world have been chosen as global messengers, and I am one of them. I will be a global messenger for two years.

During the thirtieth-anniversary year, the twelve global messengers will be the official representatives of the Special Olympics throughout the world. As a global messenger my job is to help change public attitudes to people with lerning disabilities and to make people more aware of the Special Olympics.

To do this I will give speeches to different audiences in Ireland and in other countries. I am delighted to have the chance to represent Ireland and the Special Olympics and look forward to bringing the message of the Special Olympics to more people.

In July 1998 I went with my friends Denise Judge and Caroline O'Brien to Chicago to celebrate thirty years of the Special Olympics. First we had to fly to Brussels. This is where we had our first surprise – we met Ronan and Mikey from Boyzone. Caroline spotted them first and I ran to get their autograph. When I got to Chicago I found out that my luggage had been left in Dublin. I was very upset that I would have to wait until Saturday to get it. When we arrived at the Palmer House Hotel we went to our rooms. My roommate was Stacey, from Washington State; she was really nice. The hotel was lovely, and very big. We settled in and then went for a fitting for our clothes. We were tired and so we went to bed early.

The next day Dave Lennox and Loretta Claiborne were our tutors to help us be global messengers. Loretta is a Special Olympic athlete in America. That morning was short and good. After lunch only the athletes went to

Soldier's Field. The media were there and they interviewed us. That night we had dinner on the Navy Pier, where there were beautiful water fountains. We had a great boat tour of the bay and saw the Chicago skyline by night. When we returned to the hotel I was delighted to find my luggage had arrived.

The next day we read our mission statements. Diane Levins, a media consultant, helped us improve our speeches and then videotaped us. I enjoyed this training very much because it was preparing me for my public role as a global messenger. I was so excited I ate no lunch! The makeup people, photographers and TV people arrived.

I was interviewed for the Special Olympics International and then had my official photograph taken. We had a quick trip to the Cultural Centre to run through the steps for the next day's celebration. From there we took an open-top bus ride to see all the sights of Chicago. The warm breeze was gorgeous after a long day inside. Dinner was in Planet Hollywood, where the craic was mighty. We were ready for our big day.

The next day I was excited but not nervous. We saw Tim Shriver on the TV and then had breakfast. By nine thirty we were in the lobby in our global-messenger uniforms. Everyone wanted to take photos of us! We took the bus to the Cultural Centre, where all the TV crews were waiting for our arrival. Loretto finally introduced us to the world as the twelve global messengers. Each of us delivered our mission statement and received an award. My mission statement was as follows:

My name is Rita Lawlor. I come from Dublin, Ireland. I enjoy the Special Olympics because I see all the talents of the different athletes at the Games. I think the media should pay more attention to our talents to get the public more interested in the Special Olympics.

When the Special Olympics World Games come to Ireland it could change your life too.

I learned a lot, like travelling, meeting new friends and remembering my routine in gymnastics. The best thing I have learned is how to speak to the public about the Special Olympics and I am getting lots of experience from the Special Olympics by coming here to America as a global messenger. I hope to see you in Ireland in 2003.

To our great excitement, Muhammad Ali came onto the stage and shook our hands. When the cake was wheeled in with all the candles, lighting the messengers, Eunice, Tim and Muhammad Ali blew out the candles. It was a special moment; everyone was taking photos.

After the celebration was over we had the afternoon free. We did a little shopping and then set out and had lunch. At five o'clock the coach was ready to take us to the White Sox baseball game. There was a big crowd there – 20,000 people. The global messengers were brought onto the field and introduced. We each had our names on the scoreboard: 'Rita Lawlor, Ireland'. People cheered and clapped our achievements. There was lots of fun and fireworks at the games. On the bus journey home we danced until the bus broke down! It didn't take long to fix, and soon we were home, ready for bed. Except that Laura had a surprise – there was a small goodbye party. Each of the global messengers said goodbye and thanked everyone for helping them. As a parting gift each received a signed picture of Muhammad Ali.

During breakfast the next day we searched the papers and found pictures galore. The staff in the hotel were all congratulating me. We packed our bags and headed down to the pier for a last stroll in the sun. When we returned to the hotel we quickly changed our clothes and got a taxi to O'Hare Airport. When we arrived at the check-in counter I was asked for my autograph! The lady had seen me on the evening news. Of course I gave it to her. We had a snack to keep us going and then went to the departure lounge.

Caroline made sure Denise and I got the aeroplane safely, then Caroline had to get another flight: she was going on her holidays to her mammy's in Atlanta. Denise and I were on the plane coming home to Ireland on our own. We had a good laugh.

Louise in Brussels brought Denise and myself to Dublin on 22 July 1998. Louise was interested in where I had travelled. I told her I had been in America as a global messenger.

The crew in the areoplane were very nice. They wrote this:

To whom it my concern: The Chicago Sabena staff saw Miss Lawlor while she was in Chicago. She arrrived in Chicago on SN539 and left today on SN540. She was here for the Special Olympics at Soldier's Field.

The crew all signed their names.

I showed the cabin crew my award and they thought it was beautiful. My award is made of glass and looks like crystal. I brought the American newspaper in to work to show all my friends the picture in it; they said it was lovely and I told them all about my trip and my certificates. One was for media training and the other was for being a global messenger for the thirtieth anniversary of the Special Olympics. I told them I had been on TV and they told me to put my picture on the board in work.

Even though our flight was delayed in Dublin for two hours, this was the best weekend I ever had, especially because I am now a global messenger for Special Olympics International.

Going to America wasn't my only trip in 1988. In August I went to Holland with the Special Olympics for the Together Strong conference. Shelagh Lynch, my help, and I met at twelve o'clock on 21 August. We had lots of time at the airport and the flight was fine. Volunteers at the airport drove us to Leeuwenhorst Hotel. The country is very flat: there are miles and miles of fields planted with flowers and potatoes. We saw old windmills and new ones, which generate electricity, and lots of water in the canals. At the hotel my name was spelt incorrectly so we nearly didn't have a roof over our heads! The hotel was lovely and dinner was nice – I had the best ice water I ever tasted there.

We went to an opening meeting at about eight o'clock that night. The meeting was chaired by Des Corrigan, who seems to be the main man here. He was worried that the advocates might not work enough at the workshops. The India congress three years ago was very hard work. This year there are more of us at congress. Over the last eighteen months in Europe changes took place because everyone is working for changes together. As advocates, we need to be very clear about what we want congress to hear. We will have a chance to be heard by people from all over the world.

A lady from Panama spoke about doing things for ourselves. She bent over and said that, before she made up her mind to do things, she was all crooked. Then she began to do her own things, like writing poetry and a book about herself, and she stood up tall and proud. I spoke about what I did and explained my job as a global messenger. Jackie Abraham from England thought I was brilliant and said it was a pity I was not speaking at the Inclusion international congress later that month.

The conference opened with two short speeches and then a play by a Dutch group. The play was of four people dressed in black and white sitting far apart from each other and listening to every kind of language. They looked bored and showed no interest in things. Music started. We saw the four people pull in nearer to each other and begin to dance together and work together. The play showed there is a way to work together when you get closer – 'Together Strong'.

I learned that there are people all over the world who want the same things as me. They went out and did what they wanted. By joining together we will have a stronger voice. Self-advocacy involves all of us. It means defending ourselves and making decisions. Some people need more support than others.

Jackie from England said we must work with poor people from other countries who cannot speak for themselves. Someone else said we should accept the fact that we have a disability and demand support. We should be approached in a positive way so that we can gain self-confidence. The national chairman of Inclusion, Roger Martin, said it was 'time to put the bad things behind us but not to forget!' Someone from another country said we shouldn't just complain but should do something about the problems we face. A delegate from Denmark said, 'We can do more than you imagine but we need your support.' This is what we should be telling the media. I heard one self-advocate say, 'There is money for everything but not for disability. We are undervalued.'

I was surprised to hear the words 'mentally handicapped' being used at this meeting. I think it reinforces the old idea about people like us. The media and others think, because of this way of describing us, that we do nothing for ourselves. That is not true: we have to drop this label here and now. I do public speaking about this subject and it is the reason I have written this book.

We want the media to see and write about what we *can* do in sport and life in general. I am really keen to talk about the media and to make the media recognise our talents. I was particularly looking forward to a 'Hearts and

Minds' workshop at the conference, but they did not show us any ways of getting the media to show the best side of people with disabilities.

Denmark has a weekly half-hour TV programme made by and for people with disabilities. I think this is a good idea. We need to show off our talents and ability to work. Two countries had displays of their work at the conference. I will have to put together material to show how the Special Olympics works. I feel stronger now, after the conference, about my work for the Special Olympics than I did before.

As a global messenger I was also invited to attend a Special Olympics Europe Eurasia business meeting. I travelled to Brussels and met Martha Jo Braycich, Communications and Media Relations Manager for the Special Olympics Europe Eurasia.

My main role was to give an opening speech on 23 October. I spoke about how to change public attitudes towards people with learning difficulties. It was the first time I had used PowerPoint. I was able to use pictures to help get my point across. I showed the *Change the World* video before my final slide: 'Believe in the power of sports and the power of Special Olympic athletes to change the world. As you can see we achieve our goals.'

23

THREE TRIPS I WILL NEVER FORGET

Washington, DC, USA

The fifteenth to the nineteenth of December 1998 are five days I will never forget. I went back to America as a global messenger for the Special Olympics. The goal of the Special Olympics is to give leadership jobs to more people so that they can keep improving the Games. This gives us pride in ourselves.

Geraldine Minogue, my guest, and I went shopping in a big mall a short distance from the hotel. There were plenty of Christmas things in the shops. After lunch some global messengers went on their own to the White House to meet the stars as they rehearsed. The global messengers also rehearsed and took some photos. We got ready for our big night out.

Thursday the seventeenth, the day I longed for, arrived. Over breakfast the people from the White House explained the rules, such as the times for taking photos and standing in turn. We were not allowed to hand the president anything, for security reasons. After breakfast we had a second rehearsal in the White House and then returned to the Hotel

Marriott to get ready for the real thing.

Later, back at the White House, we had a guided tour, took photos and shook hands with President Clinton as our names were called out. We were driven to the marquee on the lawns of the White House, where we had to queue up. My partner, Captain Michael R. Caffery, escorted me in. As we entered, our names were called out and we were shown to our tables. The tables were laid out beautifully for dinner.

Everything about the night was lovely. After dinner, before the show started, I got President and Mrs Clinton's autographs. During the show all the global messengers had to go out to get ready for the stage. Then we went up on the stage. I gave a speech. President Clinton was also on the stage, with his wife. I was up dancing for the last song of the night. I really enjoyed being on the stage and everyone said I was the star of the show.

At the end of the show I got the autographs of more stars, like Jon Bon Jovi, Sheryl Crow and Tracy Chapman, who had been in the show. Overall the event was a great celebration of the Special Olympics.

North Carolina, USA

We went to North Carolina for the Special Olympics World Games. On 25 June our day started with a healthy-athlete symposium at 10.45 am. The symposium was delayed so I was a good while waiting to speak. After my speech I went back at the Sheraton Imperial Hotel, where Geraldine, my guest, and I were staying. I had to prepare another speech ready for the torch run. When I had finished this speech we went to the swimming pool for a while before getting ready for the torch run reception at 7 pm. At the reception we had a disco and food.

The next day we had breakfast and then returned to the room to get ready to go to the practice session for the opening ceremonies. At 10.30 am there was a media reception, at which Geraldine and I listened to Mark, one of the global messengers, who made a speech and introduced a speaker. Then we had something to eat and there was time to have a chat.

At 1.30 pm we all went into the room where the media were waiting. Billy, another of the global messengers, gave a speech and then I got the opportunity to speak about the Special Olympics and my book. We then went back to the hotel to prepare for the founder's reception for Eunice Shriver, who set up the Special Olympics. All the global messengers were delighted to have the opportunity to meet the singer Stevie Wonder before we went to the opening ceremonies at 7 pm.

The opening ceremonies were brilliant. Mark, a global messenger, commentated on the team entering the stadium. All the global messengers were brought onto the stage with Mrs Shriver for the last song of the evening.

At 10 am on 27 June we went to the chairman's brunch, where we had some food. Mr and Mrs Shriver and Tim Shriver all spoke, and they were presented with awards. When the brunch was over we had some free time. We made our way back to the hotel, where we met up with Caroline O'Brien, the National Families Coordinator for Special Olympics Ireland. We spent the afternoon at the swimming pool before getting ready for the board of directors' dinner. The food at the dinner was really lovely and we had a great night.

The next day some of the global messengers went to a roller skating competition with the Shrivers' children. We spent some time working as volunteers, helping out with the event. I enjoyed watching the routines: they were very good and the music was nice.

In the afternoon we had some free time to go shopping, which I really enjoyed. On returning to the hotel, we had to get ready to go to the honoured-guests reception that evening.

After breakfast on 29 June Geraldine and I went to see the track-and-field competition. We were just in time to see two Irish athletes running in the 100 metres race. For lunch, we made our way back to the hotel, where we met some of the other global messengers. Sadly, we had to say goodbye to them before we headed back to Ireland that evening.

Gothenburg, Sweden
On 2 July 1999 I went to Sweden for the Eleventh World Gymnaestrada. This was a mainstream event: there was a mixture of able-bodied athletes and athletes with special needs. It was fun at the airport as we were leaving: some people had lovely banners wishing the Irish team good luck. A lot of people from the group took photos.

There were 140 athletes in the Irish team. They were from Waterford, Carmana, Tipperary, Bayside, Raheny, Clare, Sail, Ace and Northern Ireland gymnastics clubs. We all stayed in a big hotel and had nice food.

The next day the groups did their own thing. My group, Bayside, went for a walk around the city and saw where

the entertainments for the Gymnaestrada village were.
Then we went back to the school for a good while. Brigid,
one of the mothers, was going for a walk, and we went
with her. We saw the stalls for souvenirs to do with
gymnastics from different countries. Then we went back
for dinner at the famous Ullevi Stadium. I went with some
of the mammies down to the village entertainment. There
was a disco and an Abba tribute band there; we had fun.

That Sunday we had breakfast, did a practice routine
and then went for tea in the village, where there was a
band playing. We had to be back at 4.30 pm to get ready
for the opening ceremony. When all the teams had got
ready we had a photo of the Irish team taken. Then we
went down to the stadium for the opening ceremony.
There was a nice atmosphere there. We saw the teams
from other countries; there were 22,500 athletes from
forty-two countries taking part altogether. It was great
when Ireland came into the stadium. We marched in a
fantastic welcome and entertained the crowd by dancing
and doing gymnastics balances on each other's shoulders.
The routines at the opening ceremony were very good,
and it was all lovely and colourful.

Special Olympics Ireland had a stall at the conference
centre with information about the Special Olympics and
photos of the Irish team's routine. I put my global-
messenger card up on the board. I looked at some of the
information about the Special Olympics. I asked Maire, a
member of the Special Olympics committee, why the
expression 'mentally handicapped' was used in some of the
leaflets. She explained that some countries outside Ireland
would not understand the expression 'learning difficulties'.

The next day we were busy practising our routines. Bayside and Raheny gymnastics clubs performed the short routine 'Challenge the Dream'. We came back to the school to get ready to practise out major routine, 'We're Ireland, We're Special', but it was cancelled because of heavy rain.

The Bayside Gymnastics Club members went to a meeting for coaches in the conference centre. Two coaches, who were called Emer and Sinead, spoke about teaching gymnastics to people with special needs. The audience were blindfolded and the coach gave them things to feel. They felt feathers, bubbles and balls and had water squirted on them. Bayside was asked to demonstrate the equipment: we performed on the vault and the bench and did straddle jumps from the springboard. Then the coaches who were running the meeting showed a video, which said coaches should speak slowly and use simple language.

After dinner we went back to the school. Two people had their birthdays on that day, and there was a birthday cake for them. People from the Bayside club were going out. They asked me whether I would like to come out too, but it was wet and I was tired: I said 'Not!' Aoife from Kilkenny helped me with my writing.

On Thursday we had a free morning and did our own thing. I went shopping with two of the parents – Bridget and Tim – and their son Feargal. We had a good time. Then we came back to the school to get ready for the national presentation for the World Gymnaestrada. The presentation was brilliant, and it gave me ideas for how Ireland could promote the 2003 Special Olympics. For example, Australian athletes did a routine to persuade the committee to let Australia host the Special Olympics. The athletes ran and did somersaults and other types of gymnastics and at the end of the routine a person ran in with a torch. The England team also had people with learning difficulties doing their routines, and they were very good.

The next day the Ireland team went to see some Canadian people with learning difficulties. Bayside and Raheny gymnastics clubs did their 'Challenge the Dream' routine. We also practised our major routine, 'We're Ireland, We're Special', and the routine 'Together as One', which we would perform at the closing ceremony. Then we were free for the afternoon. I went back to the school and sunbathed.

After that I went with one of the parents, Ann, and her daughter Ruth to the amusement park. Then we came back and got ready for our performance of 'We're Ireland, We're Special'. We lined up outside the stadium before going in. The audience was really impressed with the routine.

Later we had dinner and got ready for the Irish night. The Ireland team went to a pub called the Dublin Bar. We had a great night: there was a disco and Irish music and it was fun. At the end of the night there was a thank-you speech for the people who had helped make the Gymnaestrada a success.

On Friday the Bayside and Raheny clubs did our last major routine: 'Challenge the Dream'. Afterwards I went swimming with Ann. Then we went to the entertainment park until nine o'clock and later we went with some of the parents down to the village, where we listened to music. It was a good night.

On Saturday we had a big Irish team photo. Afterwards Ann, her daughter Ruth and I went to the swimming pool for about an hour. I had lunch in McDonald's. Ann saw me when I was having my lunch, and when I had finished we went to the entertainment park. We only had time for one ride on the boat, but it was brilliant.

Then we went back to the school to get ready for the closing ceremony. When the Irish team was ready we went to the stadium. We all sat down and had lunch while we were waiting for it to start. It was great looking at the routines, which were very colourful. Then it was time for the Irish team to perform 'Together as One'.

Later the Swedish officials spoke and at the end the Irish team carried out the country's flag; the teams of the other countries that had performed at the ceremony did the same. The officials announced that the next World Gymnaestrada would be in Portugal in 2003. The Portuguese team then performed their routine and all the other countries joined in to celebrate together. Members of the Irish team danced in the stadium.

Afterwards Paula and I went out walking and she helped me get some swaps for badges; I swapped my global-messenger cards for the Special Olympics. I had great fun with her. Then we went back to the school for a while. Mike, Dympna and I went to the village; we just made it in time for the fireworks. The Irish team celebrated that night at a disco.

Overall, the event was a great success. Canada, Britain, Holland and Ireland, among other countries, had people with learning difficulties in their teams. Many of these people had coaches and family members with them as well. The audiences were very impressed with the performances of the athletes with learning difficulties; so were the media. The Irish team made our country proud. People with disabilities worked alongside nondisabled people in the true spirit of respect among equals: we were really 'together as one'.

*

Now that all my trips are over for the moment I have come down to earth – and gone back to my job. I have a lot of fun with my workmates: they say I'm a celebrity now and some of them ask if it's OK for them to sit beside me! The other day I was giving my workmate some gum and I asked her to slip a piece into my mouth because I had my work gloves on. She said, 'Oh yeah, we'll be feeding you as well now you're a celebrity, and pretty soon you'll have a VIP table in the staffroom all done up!'

The Special Olympics chose me to be on the commitee for the 2003 Games, which are going to be hosted by Ireland. There are two stars on this committee: Ronan Keating from Boyzone and Gerry Kelly from UTV. Over 7,000 athletes and coaches from more than 150 countries will take part in the the 2003 Special Olympics, which will be the biggest sporting and cultural event every staged in Ireland. I hope to see you all there!

People First

Everyone you meet
has a story all their own.
You are different from me
but we don't have to stand alone.

All the trouble in the world
comes from ignorance and fear.
When you look at me,
can you see the person here?

Some of us are free,
yes, and some of us are strong,
but for those still locked away
we will sing this song:

We will stand up for our rights
we will stand and tell what's true
we will show the world
all that we can do.

by Karl Williams

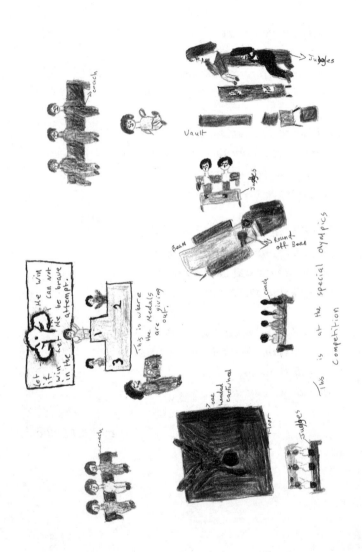

coach

Judges

Vault

Judges

Beam

Round-off Beam

Let it win he win it can not win let he be brave in the attempt.

This is where the Medals are giving out.

3 1 2

coach

This is at the special olympics competition

one handed earthwheel

Floor

coach

Judges

APPENDICES

APPENDIX 1: OUR NEEDS

Extract from a recent submission from the Dublin Self-Advocacy Group to the Forum of People With Disability on the needs of people with learning difficulties:

People with learning difficulties are not informed of their rights.

The public representatives in the Dáil are not putting enough legislation through to help the rights of people with learning difficulties. There are not enough debates in the Dáil on their rights. People with learning difficulties need to be treated the same as people who don't have learning difficulties. We are the same as you.

People with learning difficulties who need accommodation or are homeless should be housed with support workers in ordinary housing that is of an acceptable standard. There should be a lot of support, depending on need.

There should be help from the local community, like home helps.

People with learning difficulties who live on their own have a great need for emotional support – people who they can talk to and who can give them help and advice.

People with learning difficulties have a need for greater financial support, especially in relation to DPMA (disability) payments, which are felt to be too low. There should be subsidies to help independent living, more social housing provision and, especially, the provision of essentials like telephones so that people with learning difficulties can call for help if they need to.

There should be better facilities in sheltered workshops and people should receive a decent wage for the work they do.

There is a great need for access to information relating to our entitlements.

We should have a pension from our work when we retire.

People with learning difficulties need to be listened to and they should be asked their opinions more often. We should have more choices within our lives.

We should have direct representation on the executive committees of the agencies that are responsible for services to meet our needs.

APPENDIX 2:
THE DUBLIN SELF-ADVOCACY GROUP

From a submission from the Dublin Self-Advocacy Group to the Forum of People with Disability on the needs of people with learning difficulties, September 1994

The Dublin Self-Advocacy Group are seven people who are labelled 'mentally handicapped'. They meet regularly with three advisors and discuss issues affecting them and others who are disabled.

The members of the Dublin Self-Advocacy Group all live in Dublin and work in different places. Some are in sheltered workshops and others work in open in open employment while others are in training. Three of the group live alone, three live in community housing and one person lives with their family. The group has three advisors, two of whom work in services.

The Dublin Self-Advocacy Group meets to discuss issues affecting themselves and others who are disabled.

The group acts as a support group for the members and tries to develop skills in self-advocacy. In doing so it tries to develop confidence in speaking on your own behalf and on behalf of others who have also been labelled.

In being part of a self-advocacy group the members learn more about issues affecting people with disabilities and how people who are disabled can sometimes be 'walked upon'.

The group has met monthly over the last three and a half years and have worked in a voluntary capacity to support self-advocacy.

Members of the group have lobbied many other groups and organisations to promote the rights of people with disabilities.

APPENDIX 3:
HAIL, THE HOUSING ASSOCIATION
FOR INTEGRATED LIVING

HAIL was formed in 1985 as a charity and nonprofit company.

Following the production by members of the St Brendan's Mental Health Association – which is concerned with the needs of the mentally ill – of the report 'Let's Look at Housing', a group came together to establish a housing association to meet the housing requirements of persons with special needs. The group was composed of members with experience of the demand for such housing in the community, a chairman with previous experience of a housing association and Bernard Thompson, chairman of the Housing Centre.

The association aims to tackle a number of problems:

- The insecurity of tenure in the private sector for persons with special needs
- The discrimination against and lack of understanding of the needs of these people
- The difficulty experienced by local authorities in housing the single adult in areas with adequate support services

- Persons who in the past were provided with institutional care are now expected to live in the community, sometimes putting under stress other family members who find it difficult to cope with the new situation
- For those family members who do cope, this problem is deepened either by their own personal problems or, sadly, by their death. This leaves the person with special needs totally on their own and vulnerable in the community.

We are not children
we are Adults
we can speak up for
ourselves and we have
a voices